Did you enjoy this issue of BioCoder?

Sign up and we'll deliver future issues and news about the community for FREE.

http://oreilly.com/go/biocoder-news

BioCoder

SPRING 2014

O'REILLY®   Beijing · Cambridge · Farnham · Köln · Sebastopol · Tokyo

Contents

What Biotechnology Wants

Ryan Bethencourt

> *It has become evident that the primary lesson of the study of evolution is that all evolution is coevolution: every organism is evolving in tandem with the organisms around it.*

— KEVIN KELLY

We are not what we think we are.

That thought has been reverberating in my mind for many years now. As we learn more and more about ourselves, what was once classified as "junk" DNA turns out to function as gene switches, controlling facial features and likely much more. Also, our genome is filled with viral DNA, and from just what we can recognize, we have about 100,000 fragments. At least 8% of our genome is viral (we are already GMOs) and "we" are outnumbered by at least 10x by the bacterial cells that reside on and in the human body.

So what is humanity? We are biotech; we're only just now realizing the extent to which we've been altered by the biology around us.

I felt the title of this article was apt, as Kevin Kelly once wrote about how technology (and biological evolution) drove and continues to drive *Homo sapiens* development. Kelly calls that driving force the *technium*, a word designated to signify the greater global and massively interconnected system of technology vibrating around us.

Biotech wants us. It wants us to continue the path that it has started us down, changing our fundamental genetic code and adding, manipulating, and testing genes to alter ourselves and the biology all around us. It wants us to quicken the pace of change with tools evolution has already provided us with, such as the basic tools we need to cut and manipulate DNA, the source code of life. Biotech wants us to embrace it with both hands!

So what's next in biotech, and what are our tributaries? One of the best and easiest to understand classifications of biotech is based on the rainbow code of biotech. It states:

Green biotech

Agricultural biotech isn't about just your run-of-the-mill soybean genetically modified organism (GMO), but drought-resistant crops, micropropagation of different plant varieties, tools for identifying the best plants through molecular fingerprinting, and novel breeding methods (including double haploids and increased chromosome numbers). AgBio has the potential to support both current and novel needs for food, energy, and materials as humanity grows from 7 to 10 billion people.

Yellow biotech

Nutritional biotech is one of the oldest forms of biotech. It has been used to fortify foods through fermentation, creating wine, beer, cheeses, breads, and other more nutritious foods through the use of enzymes, microbes, and fungi. Many of the techniques used to create today's foods—including one of my personal favorites, sourdough bread, which was likely created in ancient Egypt and was the primary food source of marching Roman soldiers due to its nutritional content—have played a vital role in nourishing most larger human civilizations. Innovation potential in this space is still vast for new foods, flavors, and fortifications!

Red biotech

Medicine and human health, the area with which I'm most familiar, has been transformative for human health and wellness, contrary to many of the bunk science claims that anti-vaccine campaigners tout. Just in the United States, vaccines have eradicated measles, diphtheria, mumps, smallpox, and polio. Measles alone once had 500,000 yearly cases; now that number is nearly zero.

Antibiotics have been revolutionary. According to the Centers for Disease Control (CDC), "In 1900, the three leading causes of death were pneumonia, tuberculosis (TB), and diarrhea and enteritis, which (together with diphtheria) caused one third of all deaths." Forty percent of those deaths were in children under the age of five. Imagine that! Red biotech has been an overwhelming success, even making massive strides in treating and delaying diseases often associated with old age. These diseases, too, will fall to science as the power of our tools and our understanding of both genomics and human biology increases. With the announcement of Calico, a Google-backed startup aimed to combat aging-related disease, and Human Longevity Inc., formed by J. Craig Venter with the aim of sequencing and unraveling the meaning of 100k genomes per year, the race to fix the aging human body from a data-driven perspective is now beginning in earnest.

White biotech

Industrial biotechnology is a rapidly evolving space. One of the trendy new terms people have been using for industrial bio is "synthetic biology." I have to admit, I'm not really a fan. Synbio is just a new buzzword that some investors seem to be falling in love with, but the trends in industrial bio are very real and have immense potential!

This sector includes the replacement of standard industrial processes with biotech processes to create pharmaceuticals, cosmetics, food additives, chemicals, fuels, enzymes, and other materials. In many cases, this results in a decrease in the overall cost of production and increased availability of products that are harder to synthesize or refine. Two fascinating examples of industrial biotech companies moving this field forward are Plantic, which produces biopolymers and plastics based on corn, and Novozymes, which makes many of the enzymes used in laundry detergents, automatic dishwashing machines, and the food and beverage industry.

Gray biotech

This area is focused on environmental protection, which includes both premeditated efforts to protect environments, such as waste water treatment, and also efforts to remove toxins or contaminants from the environment through bioremediation, the use of microbes to degrade oil in oil spills, and the use of transgenic plants to remove heavy metals and organic contaminants from the soil.

Blue biotech

Often called "marine biotech," blue biotech refers to the harnessing of the ocean's genetic diversity through its flora and fauna. Companies like GlycoMar have developed anti-inflammatory therapies, and others like Synthetic Genomics are working on the potential of harnessing algae to create biofuels.

Gold biotech
 This field acknowledges the importance of the tools of bioinformatics and computer science in the evolution of the biotech industry. Players include software companies like DNA Nexus that are attempting to use advanced tools and cloud-based infrastructure to increase the analysis of genetic and genomic information.

 As Alan Harrington states, we must never forget we are cosmic revolutionaries, not stooges conscripted to advance a natural order.

Welcome to the beginning of the beginning of humanity's mastery of the rainbow of biology!

Ryan Bethencourt is the CEO of Berkeley Biolabs and a managing partner of LITMUS Clinical Research. He's currently working to accelerate innovations in biotechnology and medicine through biohacking, open innovation, and collaboration.

Twitter: @ryanbethencourt

Website: http://www.berkeleybiolabs.com

Beyond the Lab and Far Away: A View from Washington

Todd Kuiken

This is the first in what we hope will become a recurring series examining the governance around DIYbio, synthetic biology, and the larger citizen science movement with a focus on how Washington is engaging with the community. We encourage you to send us questions, ideas, and topics you would like to see covered in this series.

In the 1970 film *Tora! Tora! Tora!*, Admiral Isoroku Yamamoto exclaims, "I fear all we have done is to awaken a sleeping giant and fill him with a terrible resolve." This was in response to the successful 1941 attack on Pearl Harbor by forces of Imperial Japan. In spring 2013, a small project listed on Kickstarter that was part of the larger DIYbio movement awoke the US regulatory system with a dimly lit glowing plant. On May 7, 2013, *The New York Times* published "A Dream of Trees Aglow at Night" (*http://nyti.ms/1gWvrAH*), which exposed those not paying attention to the power of crowd funding and the possibilities, albeit even with a novelty product, of biotechnology and the DIYbio movement. As I opened the door to my office that morning, my phone was already blinking, the first message from a US Senator's office wanting to know how this type of product could escape regulatory oversight. As I hopped in a cab on my way up to Capitol Hill to brief the Senator's staff, all I could think about was the quote from Admiral Yamamoto. Glowing Plant's ability to raise half a million dollars in such a short period of time and the perception that there was no oversight of the first release of a genetically engineered seed produced by "amateurs" caught the government off guard. The swift and immediate reaction from the Hill gave me the sense that the "sleeping giant" had been awoken.

Our conversation was based on how a project like Glowing Plant was perceived to have escaped regulatory oversight and whether the Coordinated Framework (*http://1.usa.gov/1j86OYF*), a regulation written in the mid-1980s, was capable of dealing with applications that could come out of the DIYbio movement. Established as a formal policy in 1986, the Coordinated Framework for Regulation of Biotechnology describes the federal system for evaluating products developed using modern biotechnology. It established which federal agencies would have jurisdiction over a particular application in order to streamline the process for companies that could potentially fall under the jurisdiction of at least three federal agencies and no less than four federal laws: the Plant Protection Act; the Federal Insecticide, Fungicide, and Rodenticide Act; the Federal Food, Drug, and Cosmetic Act; and the Toxic Substance Control Act. The three main federal agencies responsible for regulating the safe use of genetically engineered organisms are the US Department of Agriculture, the US Environmental Protection Agency (EPA), and the US Department of Health and Human Services' Food and Drug Administration (FDA). As the ability to manipulate and design new organisms rapidly evolves, debates on whether the coordinated framework is suitable to regulate the changing face of biotechnology should continue. However, the issue around Glowing Plant is not whether the process it is going to use is regulated or not (*http://bit.ly/1gfoHzD*), but whether the government and general public are comfortable with "amateurs" being able to use these techniques. Glowing Plant challenges the status quo in a number of ways. First, it showed how a research project could be funded outside the traditional funding methods, how democratized access to biotechnology techniques could spur a new company with thousands of supporters, and how a project/product could be marketed and sold as an open source application. At the same time, it is challenging whether our governance structures can deal with fast-paced technologies, particularly when it comes to environmental release from products produced outside the traditional biotechnology industry.

Over the past few years, the citizen science movement has risen from a relatively unknown "underground" movement to receiving accolades from President Obama (*http://bit.ly/1d4csZ7*):

These videos show how students are imagining the future—class-rooms that are fully accessible to classmates with disabilities; individualized learning platforms that you can carry around in your pocket. And that's the kind of creativity and imagination we want all our young people to embrace. We cannot wait to see more of that innovative spirit later this year when we host our first-ever White House Maker Faire. We already have a White House Science Fair. This new event is going to highlight how Americans young and old—tinkerers and inventors—are imagining and designing and building tools and machines that will open our minds and power our economy.

— **PRESIDENT BARACK OBAMA**

This type of exposure can be both good and bad, depending on your perspective. It could potentially open the doors to federal funding, increase the ability to acquire surplus or retired laboratory equipment, and enhance access to user facilities and government expertise. However, it also shines a brighter light on the community, which could increase scrutiny from regulatory agencies and exacerbate the myths (*http://bit.ly/1oAiRgo*) that surround the DIYbio community. The movement is going to have to engage with those in the federal government if it wants to avoid knee-jerk regulatory actions based on misinformation and conjecture from a segment within the government that believes placing biology in the hands of the public is too dangerous and that the movement has nothing to contribute beyond becoming the next biosecurity threat. Anyone tinkering with and experimenting with biology raises legitimate biosecurity, biosafety, and environmental concerns. As the movement becomes more sophisticated in its scientific abilities, these concerns will continue to grow and the community should continue to address and adapt to these apprehensions.

The DIYbio movement, and the larger citizen science movement, presents an interesting dichotomy for the US government. On the one hand, it wants to support the movement (*http://1.usa.gov/PUiGku*) in order to promote innovation; on the other hand, there are legitimate biosecurity, biosafety, and environmental concerns that raise public policy and public perception issues. Like it or not, the community has a spotlight on it, and while the movement has its supporters within the government, there are those who are looking for ways to limit its ability to flourish and, in some instances, shut it down completely. By engaging directly with the government, the community can build supporters, adapt to their concerns early, and control the narrative around DIYbio.

Dr. Todd Kuiken is a senior program associate with the Science and Technology Innovation Program at the Woodrow Wilson International Centre for Scholars, where he explores the scientific and technological frontier, stimulating discovery and bringing new tools to bear on public policy challenges that emerge as science advances.

Twitter: @DrToddOliver

Website: http://www.synbioproject.org

DIYbio and Human Subjects Research

Michael Scroggins

In what follows, I am going to float a thought balloon: DIYbio laboratories should think through their relationships with Title 45 Code of Federal Regulations Part 46, informally known as the "Common Rule" (*http://www.hhs.gov/ohrp/humansubjects/commonrule/*), which establishes the existence of institutional review boards (IRBs) for research involving human subjects. I think there are two related reasons for doing so.

First, DIYbio is quickly pushing into research involving human subjects. The GETit Project (*http://getitproject.org/*) and the Immunity Project (*http://www.immunityproject.org/*) point to medical clinical research as an emerging direction for DIYbio research, and certainly there are others in the planning stage. This is not surprising, given that biology is an unusually broad discipline and DIYbio is more than just an amateur version of synthetic biology, even though it is often portrayed as such.

But medical and clinical research is a field with a long and complicated history that warrants caution. Scientists have experimented on themselves and those close to them since time immemorial. Jonas Salk, for instance, first tested his polio vaccine on himself (*http://www.jonas-salk.org/docs/InterviewFAQ.html*), then on his family, then on children at the Watson Home for Crippled Children in Sewickley, PA, then on residents of Sewickley, and then on a few traveling friends and family members. Beginning with his own body, Salk's vaccine spread outward in an ever-expanding circle.

In contrast to Salk's success, Stubbins Ffirth, an 18th-century medical apprentice, was convinced that yellow fever was not a contagious disease but rather the result of hot weather and bad temper. He "proved" his point by consuming bodily fluids produced by yellow fever patients. Luckily for Ffirth, the fluids came from patients who were no longer contagious and Ffirth survived his ill-considered experiment.[1] Unsurprisingly, Ffirth was unable to convince others to join in his experiment, leaving his a lonely circle. But, experimentation on the self and those physically and emotionally close remains at least a constant possibility, if not normal practice. Even the BioCurious motto, "Experiment with Friends," points to the ubiquity of this idea.

But there is a power discrepancy at work here. Salk and his colleagues may have understood the risks of his polio vaccine (though it is certain that Ffirth did not understand the risks of eating infected vomit), but it is less likely that Salk's family understood the risks and even less certain that the children at the Watson Home or their parents understood the risks. An IRB, in the broadest sense, is intended to protect both Ffirth from himself and Salk's family and the children of the Watson Home from Salk's enthusiasm by ensuring that everyone involved in biomedical or psychological research is fully informed about the possibility of risks and rewards at each step of the research process.

So, the IRB was established because of very real abuses in the power discrepancy between researcher and researched. The worst abuses were perpetrated by Nazi medical experiments, which led to the Nuremberg Code. But there have been many abuses carried out by otherwise well meaning but overly enthusiastic researchers. The Wikipedia page on unethical human experimentation in the United States (*http://bit.ly/1eqry9Z*) is very comprehensive on this point, so I will refer you there instead of recounting the numerous abuses here. But, keep in mind that most of the experimenters listed set out with the best of intentions.

For-Profit IRBs

Second, the recent rise of for-profit IRBs to prominence has undercut the ethical purpose of the IRB in two ways: first, by allowing IRB shopping, and second, by creating a market incentive to green-light research that would not otherwise pass. If one IRB rejects a study for being too risky, then it is a simple matter of paying another company to review the proposal until one that will green-light the project is found. The problems with for-profit IRBs have been written about in both PLOS (*http://bit.ly/1jc77NV*) and The Lancet (*http://bit.ly/1ijB2EK*), in addition to the popular press. Unlike institutional IRBs, for-profit boards have no oversight, and

---

1. Stubbins Ffirth, "A Treatise on Malignant Fever: With an Attempt to Prove Its Non-Contagious Nature" (thesis, University of Pennsylvania, 1804).

conflicts of interest involving IRB members and companies sponsoring the research before the IRB can be hidden behind the corporate veil.

The problems with for-profit IRBs were exposed by a US Government Accountability Office (GAO) sting using the fake drug Adhesiabloc (*http://1.usa.gov/OB6uE7*). Briefly, Adhesiabloc was a fake product from a fake company produced by fake researchers. The research proposal was turned down by two for-profit IRBs, but approved by a third—Coast IRB. The fake proposal described a gel to be administered post-surgery into a patient's abdominal cavity to reduce scarring by absorbing debris left after surgery. Adhesiabloc flew through the IRB process at Coast IRB, but it was not the only fake research approved (*http://bit.ly/10Asmfq*). Mercifully, Coast IRB was forced to close after the GAO investigation.

If there was ever a process (other than the patent process) that could use openness and transparency, it is the IRB. An open source IRB process is possible and would bring some welcome transparency to an often opaque system. With DIYbio already heading quickly toward human subjects research and the world of for-profit IRBs offering expensive, if not objective, reviews, now is the time for DIYbio laboratories to carefully consider establishing a relationship with the Common Rule.

Michael Scroggins is a PhD candidate in Anthropology and Education at Teachers College, Columbia University. He is currently conducting research in and around Silicon Valley on DIYbio and Citizen Science in hackerspaces and other informal institutions.

Website: http://about.me/michael_scroggins

The Parallels Between Synthetic Biology and Personal Computing

Sachin Singh Rawat

Both synthetic biology and personal computing are informational sciences. They deal with the generation, storage, and transmission of information through the animate and the inanimate, respectively. At the conceptual level, the two are very similar. Surprisingly, the parallels do not end there. Just as personal computing has dramatically altered how we do things, synthetic biology is poised to revolutionize our world even further. The similarities include:

Conceptual parallels

The basic unit of information in computing is a *bit*, which exists in only two forms: 0 or 1. In synthetic biology, it is the four nucleotide bases in the DNA. Accounting for the four nucleotides as pairs of bits—00, 01, 10, and 11—the whole human DNA can be written in just 756 MB. Proteins and genes can easily be compared to transistors and diodes as the determinants of the state of a particular reaction or passage of current. DNA repair mechanisms are similar to the error protection measures in computing. Biological data is compressed using overlapping open reading frames (ORFs). Biochemical reactions are like logic gates that use binary operations to deduce the functioning of biochemical pathways.

Ribosomes, cells, and whole tissues are increasingly being seen as operating systems, computers, and networks, which many are now tinkering with in university labs and hacker spaces. Computer programmers have taken inspiration from biology, as is evident by the development of neural networks, evolutionary selection of possible solutions, and the addition of robustness into their systems. It is time that biologists learned a few methodologies from their fellow information scientists, and some have already embarked on that process. The highly ambitious goals include writing entirely original code and developing new computers that run on similar or advanced operating systems. And by this I mean engineering novel proteins and creating new life forms similar to the ones we know—and possibly some less familiar ones, too.

Historical parallels

Computers were initially viewed as calculating giants that only large corporations, the government, or the military possessed. They became personal only in the 1980s. The two companies responsible for the paradigm shift—Apple and Microsoft—were born not out of academia or industrial establishments, but in the garages of DIY enthusiasts. Biological research has long been, and mostly still is, confined to universities and multinational institutions. In what could be a historical shift in the field, DIY biologists have sprung up over the last decade and are bringing the very same element to biology that the DIY home computer builders brought to computing. Partly, this was made possible by the ever-dropping prices of DNA sequencing and synthesis and the development of low-cost hardware.

The key elements include standardization of parts, ease of compilation, open sourcing of information (read hacker ethics), citizen involvement, and democratization of technology. It was only after these were incorporated in the garages of Silicon Valley that the computer could be placed on the desks and later in the pockets of the people. In addition to the lack of these elements, the limitations with recombinant DNA technology are that the experiments take too long and that the results are too complex to easily interpret. Synthetic biology aims to tackle these challenges and its mission can be, in my humble view, best defined as bringing engineering back into genetic engineering.

Futuristic parallels

According to some estimates, the number of mobile phones will soon surpass the number of people in the world. Computers are everywhere, and so are people who understand a thing or two about them. Teens make apps at home and start companies out of them. Nothing has ever been this personal and intuitive. Is synthetic biology following suit? What does it have to offer?

Just as anyone can learn to program, soon designing synthetic life "will be commonplace." Similar to the parallels synthetic biology has to personal computing, personal genome sequencing might lead to the engineering of systems to print customized therapeutic small molecules. But synthetic biology, specifically, has the potential to be even more revolutionary than personal computing, as it holds direct influence on the world's largest industries, namely pharmaceuticals, energy, food, warfare, and manufacturing.

As an advertisement from personal computing pioneer Apple said, "The people who are crazy enough to think they can change the world are the ones who do."

Sachin Singh Rawat is an undergraduate student at the School of Biotechnology, GGSIP University, New Delhi, India. His major interests include systems and synthetic biology, and he writes about them on his blog.

Website: http://dreamerbiologist.wordpress.com

Biotechnology Must Head for the Cloud

Sajith Wickramasekara

It's clear that the rate of hardware innovation in life science is staggering. Illumina recently made headlines by announcing it had dropped the cost of sequencing one human genome to a mere $1,000 (*http://bit.ly/OEPsEL*). While this cost excludes the much greater costs associated with data analysis and interpretation, it's still a remarkable milestone considering that the first human genome cost $3 billion to sequence just over a decade ago. That's a 3,000,000x improvement.

In contrast, the state of software is unacceptable and progressing much more slowly. How many scientists do you know who use spreadsheets to organize DNA? Or who collaborate by emailing files around? Or who can't actually search their colleagues' sequence data? If synthetic biology is going to reimagine genetic engineering, it won't be on the foundation of archaic software tools.

We need a cloud-based platform for scientific research, designed from the ground up for collaboration. Legacy desktop software has compounded systemic problems in science: poor scientific reproducibility, delayed access to new computational techniques, and rampant IT overhead. These issues are a thorn in the side of all scientists, and it's our responsibility to fix them if we want to accelerate science.

Reproducibility

The reproducibility of peer-reviewed research is currently under fire. Scientists at Amgen tried to reproduce 53 landmark cancer studies, only to find that all but 6 could not be confirmed (*http://bit.ly/1g57n2y*). Many journals do not have strict guidelines for publishing all datasets associated with a project.

Just as in life science, computer scientists care about peer-reviewed research. However, a powerful prestige economy exists around creating and maintaining open source software. If you release broken software, people will say something and contribute fixes. This feedback loop is broken in biology. It can take months for journals to accept corrections, and spotting flaws is incredibly difficult without access to all of the project materials.

Replicating this prestige economy around practical, usable output requires a culture shift. Nonetheless, that doesn't mean we can't facilitate the process. Preparing a manuscript for publication is tedious and time-consuming. Thus, there's little incentive for scientists to expend additional effort preparing and hosting project materials online after the fact. Files need to be wrangled from collaborators, data needs to be hosted and maintained indefinitely, and code used in data analysis needs to be documented. This process of "open-sourcing" a project must be as frictionless as flipping a switch.

The solution lies upstream with the software we use to actually do the work. Imagine that you plan your experiments in silico, using specialized applications for working with each type of biological data that talk to a central project repository in the cloud. Each bit of incremental progress is tracked and versioned so at any point you can jump back in time and replay your work. As you run your experiments, the hardware talks to the cloud applications in which the experiments were designed, enabling easier analysis of the results and passive note-taking that is far more comprehensive and accurate than using a lab notebook. You give your collaborators access to the online project from day one, allowing them to quickly offer suggestions and speed up research cycles. When it comes time to publish, you simply mark your project as public instead of private, and the community immediately has access to all of the work that led to your results.

Access to New Computational Techniques

Another major problem is the speed at which the latest computational techniques are disseminated. New versions of desktop software are often released on a yearly basis due to the overhead involved in developing patches and getting them installed. The upgrades are often tied to expensive license renewals, which slows uptake further. For a quickly developing field like synthetic biology, the algorithms and methods change too quickly for traditional desktop software to keep up. With web-based software, developers can easily push updates multiple times per day without any user intervention. This results in scientists getting access to cutting-edge tools without any inconvenience.

More importantly, a cloud solution would prevent the need to reinvent the wheel for each new computational technique. Imagine you devise a new algorithm for aligning DNA sequences. Any small script you write that does some data processing or analysis should not require you to go through the trouble of making sure it runs properly on your colleagues' machines. On the other hand, hosting a tool by yourself that other scientists could use would require creating your own data storage, visualization, and serving infrastructure. A shared cloud platform would provide web APIs that provide this functionality, allowing anyone with basic programming skills to develop new tools for the community.

IT Overhead

For biologists who understand that easy access to their colleagues' data facilitates more productive collaboration, the only option is often to develop a one-off database for their organization to use. Some existing products offer expensive shared database solutions, but they still require a scientific lab to obtain and maintain its own machines for running the software. The cloud should be leveraged to offer managed solutions for shared databases of biological data. Rather than having to run their own database infrastructure, scientists should be able to upload their data to an existing cloud repository, where it can be organized, searched, and quickly shared with collaborators around the world. IT will never be biologists' core competency, and moving their data from servers in their labs to the cloud would let them focus on doing biology.

The benefits of the cloud in reducing IT overhead are even clearer in "big data" applications. In many cases, biologists could clearly benefit by applying cloud technologies that the tech world has been developing for a decade. It seems ridiculous that, although bioinformatics is dependent upon having large datasets for cross-reference, simple cloud storage solutions providing easy contribution and access are not adequately used. Even when this data is available, biologists still use expensive supercomputing clusters, failing to take advantage of modern distributed techniques that make commodity hardware just as powerful. Although price may not be a significant issue for top-tier labs, the democratizing effect of cloud solutions would enable new ideas to come from anywhere. Furthermore, too many biologists are still unable to use big data because they aren't adept programmers. Cloud infrastructure could abstract away the complexity of large-scale data processing, allowing them to write simple, high-level scripts and queries that provide insight into massive datasets.

The Road Forward

A few colleagues and I were so fed up with the quality of software used in the life sciences from personal experience in research labs that we set out to solve this problem ourselves. We've made it our mission to build beautiful tools for scientists that are easy to use and take the pain out of managing and sharing biological data. Our solution is called Benchling and is currently focused on DNA. We offer a free version of our software to academics and biohackers, so I encourage you to check it out at *https://benchling.com*. Thousands of scientists are already using it to design, analyze, and share DNA, so you're in good company.

Software tends to be an afterthought in biotechnology. It's time to recognize that as scientists, whether you are a biohacker in a garage or work on a team with hundreds of scientists, you should be demanding better web-based software tools that enable collaboration and data sharing. The cloud is quickly replacing desktop software in other fields, and it provides clear benefits that should make biology no different.

Sajith Wickramasekara is a co-founder of Benchling, a cloud-based tool for designing, analyzing, and sharing biological data.

Website: https://benchling.com

DIYbiomimicry

Luis D. Rodriguez

Biomimicry is the design and production of materials, structures, and systems that are modeled on biological entities and processes (*https://www.google.com/#q=what +is+biomimicry*). For about 50 years now, scientists and engineers in the relatively young engineering field of biomimicry (*http://en.wikipedia.org/wiki/Biomimicry*) have been formally copying nature's models to improve existing machines and innovate new products. One famous example is the boxcar modeled after the box-fish (*http://bit.ly/1gfaXb9*), in which engineers copied the low drag properties of the fish to make the vehicle more energy-efficient (Figure 6-1).

Figure 6-1. Boxfish (left), box concept car (right). Photo source: http://www.greencarcon gress.com.

Biomimicry is not normally associated with the DIYbio community, as it is principally the domain of multimillion-dollar corporations and military research (*http://www.asknature.org/*) for aiding war efforts. Still, my honest endeavor to em-power as many designers, programmers, and bio artists through biomimicry as possible has initially been well received in web conferences around the world (*http://slidesha.re/1jcjSrH*).

Nature's managing of complexity and achieving of harmony can be understood with mathematical formulas beneath complicated systems. These processes have been extracted into mathematical proportions and patterns (*http://to.pbs.org/NxE5xB*) such as the Fibonacci sequence, and I dare to demonstrate its application to digital design and web programming much as scientists and engineers do with complex engineering solutions from the natural world.

When artists and designers look at nature, it's easy for them to get hung up on aesthetics. However, given the recent demand for designers to learn to program, it is now more desirable to use nature's code as expressed in mathematical arrays. Artists and designers can start by extracting "design thinking" from nature's cycles, letting that information affect the creative process, and taking chances. Ultimately, artists, designers, and programmers can make their own personal connections with nature.

"It's Pretty Much Stealing from Nature" (Joanna Aizenberg)

The Fibonacci sequence (0,1,1,2,3,5,8,13,21,34,55,89,144...), which is evident in many forms in nature, from the number of petals in a flower to the number of spirals in DNA (shown in Figure 6-2 and Figure 6-3, respectively), is a largely untapped source of art direction for digital designers and makers to literally "steal." For more information, see Joanna Aizenberg's TEDx talk, "Extreme Biomimetics" (*http://bit.ly/ 1gWNMxn*).

Figure 6-2. Various examples of the Fibonacci sequence found in flower petals. Photo source: http://www.maths.uq.edu.au/~infinity.

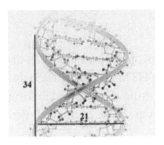

Figure 6-3. Example of the Fibonacci sequence found in DNA spirals. Graphic source: http://gold enratiomedia.com.

The same mechanisms found in the natural world to achieve beauty in organic materials, as shown above, can be applied to digital designs. Specifically dealing with box model issues (*http://bit.ly/Pff1gu*), which are at the core of the design language for laying out web applications, the Fibonacci sequence found across the natural world can save UI developers a lot of time and make interfaces feel visually and structurally "natural." Applying code from biological settings to user interfaces contributes to aesthetically pleasing, usable, cross-device user experiences. See Figure 6-4 for an example of a box model.

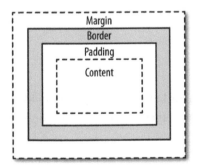

Figure 6-4. Box model diagram consisting of content, padding, border, and margin, which affect the proportions of web page elements. Graphic source: http://www.w3schools.com.

A Practical Example

A tile interface is a common way to present atomic units of information. This tutorial covers how to build a bare-bones tile interface using HTML5/CSS3/JavaScript and assumes you have basic web design skills such as writing markup and linking external files. However, source code for this example is available at the codePen (*http://codepen.io/uxcodeine/pen/cLpsq*).

 All JavaScript in this example uses jQuery and should be included in a snippet in the body after jQuery has been loaded.

Set up an array of numbers that will contain the first 18 digits of the Fibonacci sequence:

```
fibArr = [00, 01, 01, 02, 03, 05, 08, 13, 21, 34, 55, 89, 144, 233, 377,
610, 987, 1597];
```

Insert (or append) into the DOM a `div` element (or tile) for each digit in the Fibonacci sequence with jQuery's each function:

```
$.each(fibArr,function(){
   $('body').append('<div></div>')
});
```

Set the initial dimensions of each tile based on the box model properties (width, padding, border, and margin—fw, fp, fb, and fm, respectively) corresponding to the first four places in the Fibonacci array:

```
var fw = 1
var fp = 2
var fb = 3
var fm = 4
```

Next, implement an event handler (*http://bit.ly/1llPAVt*) that iterates through the array in sets of four ([00,01,01,02]...[08,13,21,34]...[377,610,987,1597] ...) and increases or decreases the values using the operands ++ or --:

```
fw++ || fw--
fp++ || fp--
fb++ || fb --
fm++ || fm--
```

In the same event handler, modify the style properties of the tiles using jQuery's css method:

```
$('div').css({
  width: fibArr[fw],
  padding: fibArr[fp],
  borderWidth: fibArr[fb],
  margin: fibArr[fm]
})
```

Watch the tile layout adapt by iterating through fibArr when the handler is invoked by HTML events in Figure 6-5, Figure 6-6, and Figure 6-7.

Figure 6-5. Interface tiles at [08,13,21,34].

Figure 6-6. Interface tiles at [377,610,987,1597].

Figure 6-7. Interface tiles at [00,01,01,02].

These figures show just one simple way to solve a common problem for an HTML5 web interface using a mechanism "stolen" from biological settings. It's an approach to expedite development that looks to an organic design language that has been adapting across different environments for aeons. A more detailed explanation and source code for this and other examples of animation, grid systems, and JavaScript functions are available in the codePen collection "Fibonacci Sequence in Open Web Standards" (*http://codepen.io/collection/Izdwx*).

As artists, designers, programmers, and strategists look ahead, there is a lot to be defined and discovered in systems aiming to develop organic user interfaces[1] and find solutions to the world's most pressing problems. Intently observing the natural world and embracing its interconnectedness can give us a lot of innovative ideas for design, bio art, and beyond.

Luis D. Rodriguez grew up in Ecuador, South America, surrounded by nature, and now lives in the Washington, DC metropolitan area. He combines his background in graphic design with training in screenwriting to complement his web development and interaction design skills. An avid user interface prototyper, he keeps up with all the latest trends and developments and is active in design and UX conferences around the world.

Twitter: @uxcodeline

[1]. Rachel Hinman. "The Emergent Mobile NUI Paradigm," in *The Mobile Frontier: A Guide to Designing Mobile Experiences.* (New York: Rosenfeld Media, 2012.)

Hacking Lab Equipment

Peter Sand

A typical biology lab is filled with dozens of machines that each function independently. Our goal is to find ways for the machines to interoperate. In this article, we will demonstrate how to create simple electronic interfaces for different kinds of devices so that they can be controlled and coordinated by a computer.

Hacking traditional lab equipment provides a way to incrementally introduce automation into your workflow. You do not need to clear out space for a large, expensive robot that might be more cumbersome than useful. You can gradually add more automation in a way that coexists with manual processes.

Automation has the potential to improve reproducibility by increasing procedural precision and providing new experimental capacity that can be allocated to validating previous results. However, the form of automation is important: an experiment designed around a $200,000 robot may not be easy for an outsider to reproduce. Instead we propose to create experiments designed around the automation of commodity hardware.

For this approach to improve reproducibility, we will need good documentation. We should support equipment manufacturers that provide easy-to-use, easy-to-hack electrical and software interfaces suitable for automation. Open equipment documentation will become an important component of open science.

Our Approach

We will take a do-it-yourself, but not do-everything-yourself approach. If we spend all our time building equipment, we won't have time to use the equipment, so rather than building devices from scratch, we'll modify standard lab equipment. (If you'd like to build your own lab equipment from scratch, check out Tekla Labs (*http://www.teklalabs.org/*).)

We won't yet address a big part of lab automation: liquid handling. A computer-controlled centrifuge isn't going to do much good unless you load something into it. An automatic pipettor isn't very useful if it is stationary. We'll cover liquid handling in another article.

Even without liquid movement, hacking these devices can be useful. You can have your computer keep a log of the parameters for every centrifuge run. You can make a semiautomated system that alternates between machine actions and human actions. You can create a computerized lab partner that guides you through a complex procedure so that the results are more consistent.

Even focusing on hacking traditional lab equipment, we can consider several approaches:

1. Using servos or other actuators to turn knobs and push buttons (this is safer than other approaches because we don't need to modify equipment internals, but engineering reliable mechanical connections is difficult)

2. Replacing the buttons and knobs with electrically controlled devices (relays, digital potentiometers)

3. Replacing the entire control system with a new control system, only keeping the mechanical components

We choose option 2, since it requires the least engineering work. With sufficient care, it can be reliable and reversible.

Safety

These projects will probably void your warranties and could quite possibly destroy your equipment. You could electrocute yourself or burn down your lab building.

Make sure the equipment is unplugged before you open it. Even then, proceed with caution; unplugged electronics may still hold a dangerous charge.

If you buy used equipment, you should consider the possibility that it is biologically or chemically contaminated. These machines are generally not autoclavable, though some may have autoclavable components.

Getting Started

We assume that you have a soldering iron, a multimeter, and a microcontroller such as the Arduino. You can find many tutorials for these tools online.

The Grove system by Seeed Studio includes various sensors and other components that can be easily attached to an Arduino. Grove devices connect with a four-conductor cable that provides power (typically 5V), ground, and two data lines. For expediency, we'll use a combination of the Grove system and breadboarding, but the Grove system is not required; all of these circuits can be built using only wires and bare components.

Additional instructions and photos for these projects are online at *http:// www.modularscience.com/doc*.

Hacking a Centrifuge

The Revolutionary Science RS-102 is a simple, inexpensive centrifuge. A rotary switch selects between four modes: off, pulse, 6,000 RPM, and 10,000 RPM. The pulse mode will run at 10,000 RPM as long as the switch is held in that position.

Inside the machine, you'll find a large motor and a circuit board attached to the rotary switch. Use a screwdriver to pry off the switch cover. Remove the screws behind the cover to free the circuit board.

Number the switch terminals 1 to 4 in clockwise order when looking at the front of the switch (Figure 7-1). Terminal 2 receives a rectified 120V AC input voltage. Terminal 3 is connected to the input when 6,000 RPM is selected. Terminals 1 and 4 are connected to the input when 10,000 RPM is selected. Solder wires to the terminals and connect them to a pair for relays. We'll use standard Grove relays; they are rated to 15A at 120V. Make sure that your wire is also rated for this current and voltage and that the high-voltage connections to the relays are well insulated.

Use digital outputs from your microcontroller to activate the relays. One output will operate the centrifuge at 6,000 RPM and the other will operate it at 10,000 RPM. Activating both relays at once is not a problem; this will simply bypass the resistors used for the slower speed, resulting in 10,000 RPM operation. When both relays are off, the manual controls will operate normally.

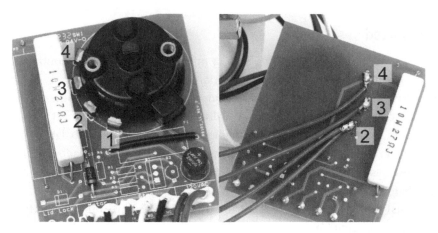

Figure 7-1. We connect wires to the centrifuge control switch so that it can be activated using relays.

Hacking a Stir Plate

The Corning PC-420D is one of the most common stirring hot plates. It has two knobs on the front: one to control temperature and one to control stirring speed. Each knob also acts as an on/off switch. Inside you'll find a few circuit boards and a motor. A metal plate on the motor functions both as a cooling fan and as part of an optical encoder that measures the speed of the motor.

Our task is fairly simple: we want to have a computer turn the knobs. Fortunately, the knob connections are easily accessible on one of the internal circuit boards. Each knob has five terminals: two operating as a switch and the other three as a standard potentiometer. We will replace each switch mechanism with a relay and each potentiometer with a digital potentiometer.

Viewing the board as shown in Figure 7-2, the left side of the potentiometer is low (ground) and the right side is high (about 3V). Remove the board and clip the middle lead on each potentiometer. (This can be reversed later by soldering.) Solder wires onto the back of the circuit board as shown.

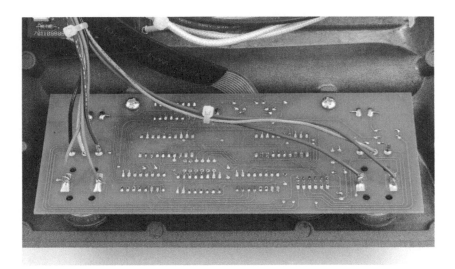

Figure 7-2. Manual controls on a stirring hot plate are replaced with devices controlled by software.

We will use a DS1803 dual digital potentiometer with a 10k ohm range. (The original potentiometers have a 1.3k ohm range, but we do not need a perfect match since they are acting as voltage dividers; in fact, we could probably use a digital-to-analog converter for this application.) Connect the physical potentiometer's low, high, and wiper (middle) leads to the DS1803's low, high, and wiper pins. Connect the GND, VCC, SDA, and SDL pins to the microcontroller (for example, using a Grove cable plugged into an I^2C port on a Grove shield). You will also need to tie the microcontroller ground to the low end of the potentiometers. Once fully connected, the microcontroller can send I^2C commands to the DS1803 to digitally turn the knobs. The original potentiometers are no longer functional.

One remaining task is determining the relationship between potentiometer values and the RPM and temperature settings. Our approach is to manually test a set of key values and perform the corresponding mapping in software. Alternatively, you could decode values from the seven-segment displays or from the control circuitry.

Hacking an Electronic Pipette

The Eppendorf Xplorer is a standard electronic pipette. It contains a small linear actuator that drives the pipette's aspiration and dispensing. An LCD shows a menu system for changing the pipette volume and other parameters.

To automate this device, we will have our microcontroller perform button presses. For simplicity, we use Grove relays to activate each button. Solid-state relays or transistors are reasonable alternatives. Unfortunately, the tip ejector is manual; it can be controlled electronically by adding an external linear actuator (for example, from Servo City).

To open the pipettor, first remove the tip ejection button, then carefully squeeze the sides to remove the front cover. Inside you will find two small push buttons corresponding to the up and down directions and two smaller buttons for the left and right options. Solder wires onto the up and down buttons as shown in Figure 7-3. Be careful that you don't apply too much heat to the circuit board. Connect the wires to a pair of relays, each attached to a digital output from your microcontroller.

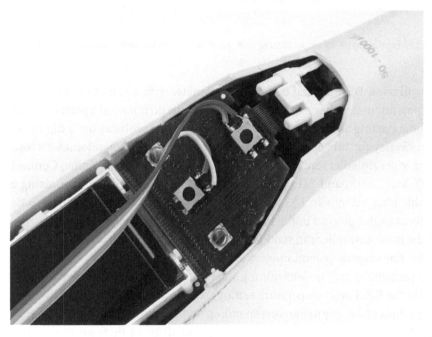

Figure 7-3. The buttons on an electronic pipette can be triggered using a microcontroller.

The up and down buttons are sufficient for triggering the aspiration and dispensing actions. If you'd also like to set the capacity electronically, add relays for the left and right buttons. This will require that the microcontroller blindly navigate the menus.

Ideally, we would obtain feedback about the current settings rather than navigating blindly. One crazy option is using computer vision software and a camera pointed at the display. A better alternative would be direct control via the pipette's USB port, a subject for future hacking.

Conclusion

We have described approaches that can be used to automate a variety of basic lab machines. Almost anything that is controlled by buttons and potentiometers (as opposed to mechanical levers or a computer) can be automated using these building blocks.

To apply this approach to other equipment, you'll need to carefully determine the voltage and current levels for the original electronic controls and choose replacement electronics accordingly. Make sure that you understand the circuits before modifying them. Use a multimeter and visually follow circuit board traces. Always be especially cautious with high voltages.

Controlling lab devices is only one part of lab automation. You will likely want to add movement: loading plates, moving vials, and multi-location pipetting. You will also need software to control all of this. We'll cover these topics in upcoming articles.

Peter Sand is the founder of Modular Science, a company building new tools for lab automation. He also founded Manylabs, a nonprofit focused on science and math education. He has a PhD in Computer Science from MIT and a BS in Computer Science from Carnegie Mellon.

Twitter: @modularscience

Website: http://www.modularscience.com

Fun and Fights with Fungi, Part I

Derek Jacoby

This was supposed to have been a nice little article on barcoding mushrooms. There was a simple protocol, and lots of folks in the DIYbio community have done all sorts of barcoding so it should have just gone easily, right? Well, not really. Unlike debugging computer code, where everything is right there to see, when debugging biology there's a whole lot of inference involved. So even though I don't have a huge set of exciting mushroom barcoding results to share, I thought sharing my experiences so far might be of some general interest.

This story starts back in October 2013 when *BioCoder* contributor Noah Most ("*Interview with Ian Marcus of SynBio4All*") was visiting Victoria, BC, Canada. I dragged him and my friend Andy around to a few of the mushroom shows that spring up in the fall in British Columbia. The goal was to take pieces of the mushrooms on the show tables, which had already been identified by experts, and do a genetic identification. This would result in one of three possibilities. First, the mushroom could exist in the barcoding database and agree with the expert identification. Yay, concordance! Second, the mushroom could exist in the database, but be different than what the expert identified. This would also be interesting. Finally, the mushroom could be absent from the barcoding database, meaning we could put it in! That's the really fun part, when something I've discovered turns out to be new and adds to our shared pool of scientific knowledge.

So where's this barcoding database? And how does this all work? DNA barcoding is a process of using a predefined section of an organism's DNA to identify it. Different kingdoms use different segments of DNA—the barcode region for animals is not the same for plants, which is not the same for bacteria. But in each case, the concept is the same. The barcoding region is an area of the genome that is not under evolutionary selection pressure, so over evolutionary time it is subject to random drift. This means that each species you want to identify will have random variations in the barcoding region. As more species are collected into the barcoding database, it becomes possible to construct a phylogenetic tree of the species based on genetic similarity. The central place on the Web for DNA barcoding (*http://www.barcodeoflife.org*) covers a lot of things we're not directly interested in for fungal barcoding, so we use a more specific site (*http://www.fungalbarcoding.org/*).

One of the first things that must be done in barcoding is to identify the set of primers that will be used. Since we want to use a small segment of the genome and not have to sequence more than we need to, the first step in barcoding is to extract that DNA from the fungal cells and amplify our barcoding region using polymerase chain reaction (PCR.) The primers determine which region it is that we will amplify. Originally choosing the primers in fungi took a lot of work and a lot of cross-species comparison. Through the process, a number of different barcoding regions were suggested. The most common barcoding region currently used is between locations ITS1 and ITS4, so we'll use primers ITS1F and ITS4R to amplify our barcoding region, leaving us only approximately 800 base pairs to be sequenced. (A more detailed look at other fungal barcoding regions is available online (*http://bit.ly/PUjeqn*).

But I've skipped over a part, and it's a part that needed a lot of debugging. How do you extract the DNA from the fungal cells? Many of you have probably seen the demonstration of getting DNA from a strawberry—if not, it's a great instructional activity and a lot of fun. There's a complete protocol online (*http://1.usa.gov/1gWxogq*). Unfortunately, most fungi are not as easy as strawberries. Trying to extract DNA with the dishwashing detergent, salt, and water mix that works well on strawberries isn't effective on most fungi. This step of the DNA prep consists of breaking the cell open—through mechanical and chemical means with a lysis buffer—then precipitating the proteins and spinning down the precipitate in a centrifuge (this leaves the DNA in the supernatant—the liquid on top of the pellet of protein). Then, with the proteins gone, you perform an isopropanol extraction of the DNA and an ethanol wash. Finally, the DNA is rehydrated and ready to be used. I started out trying to use the cell lysis buffer from a Carolina Biological barcoding kit, but that seemed to be a protocol geared mostly toward plants, and none of the first three mushrooms I tried in that protocol produced any template DNA. Frustrated, I ordered a DNA prep kit from Feldan (kit number 9K-006-0016) and tried that. It still didn't work very well. Finally, using the cell grinding and mechanical disruption from the Carolina kit and the lysis buffer from the Feldan kit, I began to get results—at least, from some of the mushrooms. There remain some mushrooms that I am not very successful in getting DNA out of: specifically, the ascomycetes, which include mushrooms such as morels, seem to be very resistant to DNA extraction using this protocol. In the end, I suspect I will have to use more forceful mechanical disruption techniques, perhaps sonication or something else that would release more DNA. I would also like to find a cheaper DNA prep solution—perhaps guanidine for a lysis buffer instead of depending on kits that end up costing 75 cents or so per prep.

If all has gone well in the DNA extraction, you see an 800-base pair band when you run a gel of the PCR product. (Running a gel consists of pulling negatively charged DNA through a gel matrix using electrical potential in order to sort the DNA fragments by size.) Before sending things away for sequencing, it's important to verify that you have produced a nice sharp band on the gel, indicating that the barcoding region was properly amplified. Here was the place where a second round of debugging was needed. Gel electrophoresis is a basic procedure that is used in all sorts of molecular biology, including protein and DNA identification. When using gel electrophoresis for identifying DNA fragments, you generally run a lane of the gel with a size standard. This is known as a DNA ladder, and allows you to compare your unknown DNA fragments with DNA fragments of known size. When I ran the first gel I didn't see anything, not even the ladder DNA. This told me that something was wrong with my gel.

Historically, gels have been run using a DNA binding dye called ethidium bromide (EtBr.) It's very effective, but EtBr is a mutagen and requires hazardous waste disposal, so most labs try to move away from using it. One of the gel dyes that I like is called GelGreen (*http://bit.ly/1iHavSu*), but it had been a few months since I last used my stock of GelGreen. Apparently it is not as shelf-stable as would be ideal. When I saw nothing, I ran a gel on EtBr and at least saw my ladder bands, so I knew something was there. One of the other folks in the lab, Vince, had the bright idea to use a UV laser (405 nm) to excite the GelGreen rather than the set of blue LEDs that we normally use. When viewed through an orange filter, the laser illumination let the dim bands pop out, whereas they were not visible at all under our normal illumination. We ordered new GelGreen and will go back to our normal gel procedures soon, but maybe we'll get Vince to write up an article on his super-sensitive laser gelbox in a future *BioCoder* issue. Seeing the ladder bands gave me confidence in the lack of amplification of the samples and led me back to debugging either the PCR process or the DNA extraction process, and concluding in this case that it was an extraction problem.

At this point I have a couple species of mushroom sent off for sequencing, but no results yet (see Figure 8-1). The experts identified them as *Sparassis crispa* and *Pseudohydnum gelatinosum*, but we'll see if that's what they really are. Then there are about 40 more samples to run through that we collected from the mushroom shows. We'll go through the bioinformatics in the next issue, after I get results back. My current passion happens to be fungi, but DNA barcoding is applicable to any living organism you might be interested in. I bet there are new discoveries to be made right in your backyard!

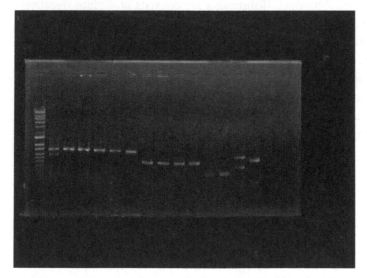

Figure 8-1. Gel electrophoresis of the two samples, Pseudohydnum gelatinosum and Sparassis crispa, in lanes 13 and 14. S. crispa is showing a double band and had to be rejected for sequencing, but P. gelatinosum was properly identified by sequence results.

Derek Jacoby spent a decade at Microsoft Research and is now a PhD candidate at the University of Victoria focused on biological data analysis. He also runs a community biology lab called biospace.ca and has been a participant and mentor on several iGEM teams.

Website: http://biobit.ca/biospace

Interview with Ian Marcus of SynBio4All

An Open, Online Platform for Collaboration on Synthetic Biology Projects

Noah Most

"We all have ideas," Ian Marcus, the project leader of SynBio4All (*http://synbio4all.org/*), told me as we sat down at the Citizen Cyberscience Conference 2014 (*http://cybersciencesummit.org/*), "but why is it that the only people that can come up with ideas are people that have been very myopic in their research?"

While many citizen science programs channel that spirit, top-down initiatives dominate the largely academic-led citizen science landscape. Typically, laypeople are limited to either collecting data (eBird (*http://ebird.org/content/ebird/*)) or recognizing patterns (WhaleFM (*http://whale.fm/*)). Many initiatives define citizen science as merely a way for citizens to help scientists. Although these top-down initiatives have yielded many exciting results, including more than 50 publications (*https://www.zooniverse.org/publications*) out of the Zooniverse citizen science portal (*https://www.zooniverse.org/*), there has been comparatively little support by academics to affirm citizens' capabilities *as* scientists—able to develop interesting ideas, design valid protocols, and interpret results.

SynBio4All, developed at the Paris Descartes University, aims to help change that. "SynBio4All is an open, online, collaborative platform by which citizen scientists, DIYbiologists, and academics could take a project from start to finish," Marcus explained. "They come up with the idea, they design the project, they help with the lab work if they want, and they disseminate the results to the public. And all of it is open, online, and for everybody to see."

Part massively open online course (MOOC) for synthetic biology, part open laboratory notebook, and part discussion platform, SynBio4All aspires to be a hub for people to learn about synthetic biology and collaborate on open science projects. Anyone, Marcus said, can float an idea on the platform and the community can help build a research plan, aid in the interpretation of results, and even "take [the idea] in a totally different direction."

Marcus wishes that such a platform had existed while he worked on his PhD. "I didn't know who to talk to and there was no real communication with anyone. It would have been nice to have just this type of platform on which I could say, 'Has anyone thought about this technique before?' I found that in the academic lab, things were very closed. We didn't want to get scooped. You didn't want to totally say exactly what research you were doing."

The plan is for the research process to be broken down so that beginners are not immediately turned off from the experience. "We don't want to overwhelm everyone up front, so everything is done in a very digestible manner."

If successful, Marcus hopes that a learning-through-research model will demonstrate a "new style of pedagogy," so that ultimately children, "born scientists," do not have their natural inclinations to experiment "[taken] away from them in this almost factory setting of schools."

With more individuals—both newcomers and veterans—participating in an open process, Marcus wants to improve science itself. "There's a lot of stuff that we can all share, there are a lot of techniques that a lot of people know that others don't know, and there are a lot of ideas out there. Bringing it all together in one place could perhaps maximize our efficiency."

However, not every part of the platform is complete: the design plan and project pages are under construction. Perhaps the biggest question is how many citizens will show up. The SynBio4All team would love to see iGEM teams, would-be iGEM teams without funding, and DIYbiologists use their platform.

While Marcus noted that some counter-cultural elements of DIYbio seek to demonstrate that "we don't need academics," he hopes that by providing a useful communication tool he can "bring the counter and culture together."

If that fails, perhaps the allure of top-notch equipment, project funding, and a lab bench might help. SynBio4All offers a unique pathway for nonprofessionals to land a bench and funding at a synthetic biology lab (*http://synbio4all.org/about-our-lab/*) at Paris Descartes University.

"We're going to end up having two projects come to our lab" from the platform between June and August, Marcus explained. This lab can support projects both this year and the next. If all goes well, the program will be continued. Moreover, by allowing citizens to showcase their projects on the platform, Marcus hopes to make others in academia more willing to collaborate with citizens in the future.

Noah Most has been hopping around the globe exploring DIYbio on a Thomas J. Watson Fellowship. He recently graduated from Grinnell College in Iowa, where he studied biology, economics, and entrepreneurship.

Twitter: @mostnoah

Community
Announcements

SynBioBeta

SynBioBeta is launching two new courses: "Introduction to Carbon Central Metabolism" and "Big Data for Synthetic Biology: An Introduction to Bioinformatics." You can learn more about each course at *http://synbiobeta.com/courses*. These will all be taught in the Bay Area, California. If you would like to host these courses in your city, then please get in touch. A variety of course options can be customized for your organizational needs.

Introduction to Carbon Metabolism (April 17, 2014)
> This course is an introduction to fundamental keys and concepts of central metabolism as relevant to synthetic biology and metabolic engineering. We begin by discussing metabolites as requirements for life to exist and give a birds-eye view of the major pathways cells use to fulfill those requirements. We discuss general thermodynamic principles in biological systems, microbial fermentation, and microbial respiration. We will analyze metabolic pathways on the basis of carbon use, ATP use, and redox balance. After learning these skills, we will identify advantages and disadvantages of possible synthetic biology routes to common household products and chemicals of the biotech industry.

Big Data for Synthetic Biology: An Introduction to Bioinformatics (April 24, 2014)
> You will learn the basics of bioinformatics, a multidisciplinary field with specializations that include interpreting human genetics, developing new medicines, and uncovering the underlying mechanisms of cellular function. We will start with a general introduction to the field as a whole, and then dive in with a number of hands-on examples where you will assemble a miniature "reference" genome, evaluate a disease-causing genetic mutation, and assess the success of sample drug trial results. Through these examples, we will uncover

the principles behind genome sequencing, interpretation of expression data (RNA-seq and arrays), and personalized medicine. Finally, we will cover introductory statistics (which will be required for interpreting data) and the potential ethical implications of applied bioengineering.

Genspace

3-Day Intro to Synthetic Biology (April classes; schedule at http://www.genspace.org)
Never clone alone...join the class and build a color-generating microbe using the Genomikon system. Synthetic biology is the science of engineering living organisms as if they were biological machines. You'll learn how to manipulate life using standardized genetic parts. These genetic sequences serve as building blocks in the fabrication of genetic "circuits," previously unseen in nature. Among many applications, this rapidly maturing technology is currently being harnessed to cheaply create life-saving drugs, biofuels to reduce dependence on petroleum-based fuel sources, and biosensors to detect a wide variety of environmental pollutants and pathogens . As part of this very hands-on course, we'll build a set of DNA "parts" into a plasmid using the Genomikon kit and load it into bacteria. We will also analyze pathways that enable engineered microorganisms to smell like bananas and respond to different genetic "instructions."

Berkeley Biolabs

We are launching many new courses! Join us at *http://www.meetup.com/Berkeley-Biolabs/.* Courses being offered include:

Biomedical tech open hack nights (late April/early May)
Sponsored by the UC Berkeley Bioengineering team.

Building Biotechs (May)
An ongoing series with speakers from the industry who discuss leaving academia, funding their biotechs, and the process of building their biotechs (please feel free to see our previous speakers).

Playing with Plasmids and Open Biohack night (every Monday)
Every Monday night, come and play with plasmids. Learn how to use the tools of bioinformatics and wet biology to make molecular parts for the Golden Braid system and other molecular machines.

Bio art project: Tree of Knowledge (starting in May)
This Burning Man–funded bio art project involves making a glowing tree. Come and help us create an amazing project for the playa at Burning Man (*http://www.burningman.com/on_the_playa*) with an amazing global group of volunteers: a cross-team collaboration between artists, makers, academics, and builders from Harvard University, UC Berkeley, UCSF, Stanford, Creative Commons, the Open Design + Hardware Network at the Open Knowledge Foundation, Berkeley Biolabs, Counter Culture Labs, BioCurious, and the Open Tech Collaborative.

BIOHACKERS IN RESIDENCE

We are currently recruiting for our inaugural class of Biohackers in Residence, and we would love for you to apply. The program will provide free access to Berkeley Biolabs in exchange for supporting the lab with volunteer hours! The Hacker in Residence volunteers are trained in molbio techniques and are invited to be involved in BBL internal projects. If you are local to BBL and are interested, send us a brief biographical sketch and a description of your interests (*http://berkeleybiolabs.com/contact-us/*).

COMPANIES CURRENTLY INCUBATING AT BERKELEY BIOLABS

Beyond Berlin
Aaron Berliner and his team are building exciting bioremediation and therapeutic technologies.

Valen
Jayaranjan Anthonypillai and his team are creating a biomass processing company for waste and cultivated streams to create specialty chemicals, fuels, and consumer products.

More coming soon!

Lightning Source UK Ltd.
Milton Keynes UK
UKOW06f1912170414

230142UK00010B/42/P